FORTY DAYS
OF PRAYER:
The Power of a Praying Church

A Daily Devotional
& Group Study Guide

by Scott Hagan

with Andrew S. Mason & Jason Yarbrough

CONTENTS

Welcome to 40 Days of Prayer!

<u>The Lord's Prayer</u>
(Matthew 6:9-13 New King James Version)

⁹Our Father in heaven,
Hallowed be Your name.
¹⁰ Your kingdom come.
Your will be done
On earth as it is in heaven.
¹¹ Give us this day our daily bread.
¹² And forgive us our debts,
As we forgive our debtors.
¹³ And do not lead us into temptation,
But deliver us from the evil one.

What would happen if a church spent 40 days seeking God through the Lord's Prayer? What would be different about your life if a handful of believers prayed for you every day for six weeks straight? What could Jesus do in a faith-filled environment such as this?

For a good part of my life, no one ever challenged me to pray. When I was 20 years old, a man in my church named Joe Elston invited me to regularly pray with him at 6 A.M. Not only was it the first time anyone had challenged me to pray, it was also the first time anyone had made time to pray with me. I would never be the same.

Just as I had someone to pray with, I encourage you *NOT* to go through this study alone. Use this study with a small group of friends to enhance your *40 Days of Prayer* journey. In each video session, I will remind you to pray for the members of your group everyday.

As we raise-up a standard of prayer in our lives, we will look to the Lord's Prayer as our guide. This is not only Jesus' model for prayer given to His disciples, but it's also the daily components of the Christian life.

For the next six weeks we will bombard the heavens with prayer and expectancy for each other. We will talk about the power of prayer and its essential ingredients. The Bible says, "The earnest prayer of a righteous person has great power and produces wonderful results" (James 5:16 *New Living Translation*). My desire for my life, your life and every member of the body of Christ is that we would be people marked by a lifestyle of prayer. So, for the next 40 days your attention will be shifted, refocused and fixed toward the throne of God through prayer.

This study guide includes four components:
1. Group curriculum that allows you to follow along for each group session
2. Scripture memory verses for each week
3. A 40-day devotional for daily reading and inspiration. Each devotion includes a short prayer to launch your prayer time for the day.
4. Designated space for daily journal entries

What would happen if a church spent 40 days seeking God through the Lord's Prayer? Let's find out together!

Scott Hagan

Session 1: OUR FATHER

WELCOME

Each week, give people 5-10 minutes to find your location and arrive. If possible, provide light snacks and have upbeat Christian music playing in the background until you officially begin your group meeting.

CHECKING IN

1. **INTRO:** If this is your group's first meeting or if you have new group members, be sure to introduce yourselves. Review the Small Group Guidelines on page 117 of this study guide.

2. **ASK:** How do you want to grow from this *FORTY DAYS OF PRAYER* study?

MEMORY VERSE

For you did not receive the spirit of bondage again to fear, but you received the Spirit of adoption by Whom we cry out, "Abba, Father."

Romans 8:15 NKJV

VIDEO

3. **WATCH:** Play the Session 1 video. Scan the QR Code or go online to:

scotthaganleads.com/40-days-of-prayer

DISCUSSION QUESTIONS

(Please don't feel pressured to discuss every question. It's okay to choose the questions that are right for your group. The point is not to race through the session; the point is to take time to let God work in your lives)

4. **ASK:** What is a common distraction that can keep us from praying consistently?

5. **READ ALOUD:** Have everyone open their Bibles to Matthew 6:9-13 and have someone read it out loud.

6. **READ ALOUD:** It's interesting that Jesus began the Lord's Prayer with calling upon God as "Our Father." In the video, Scott talked about how the presence of his earthly father activated his confidence. Praying to our heavenly Father should activate our confidence even more so.

7. **ASK:** If we knew that prayer would activate our confidence in a significant way, would we pray more than we currently do? Explain.

8. **READ ALOUD:** In the video, Scott said, "When we have messed-up earthly fathers, it messes up our view of our heavenly Father."

9. **ASK:** What baggage do you carry around with you? How do you think this affects your prayer life?

10. **READ ALOUD:** Scott said, "This isn't about our view of God; it's about God's view of us." Imagine praying and worshiping with a healthy disposition to our heavenly Father. Imagine feeling good about how He sees us as a son or daughter.

11. **ASK:** How does praying and worshiping with the *Father's view of us* bring healing to your wounded heart?

PRAYER

If more than eight people are in your group, we recommend you break into subgroups of three or four people by gender. This will give everyone ample time to share and pray together. If praying in a group is new or uncomfortable for you, we encourage you to start by praying single-sentence prayers. Don't worry about how fancy you sound. God isn't looking for eloquence. He just wants honesty. Talk to God like you talk to a friend. Give everyone a chance to pray, but don't insist on it. Over time, you will all feel much more comfortable praying together.

12. **PRAYER REQUESTS:** Ask for everyone's prayer requests. Encourage everyone to briefly share their requests so you can spend more time praying for your requests than talking about them. Be sure to record them on the Small Group Prayer and Praise Report on page 119 of this study guide. Commit to pray for each other's requests every day this week. Once all the requests are gathered, move into a group prayer time.

13. **OPTIONAL:** Once you've gathered all prayer requests, play a worship song—before you pray—from a stereo or MP3 player (if your setting allows for this). If you have the song lyrics on sheets, you may pass them out. If not, encourage people to listen to the words if they're not familiar with the song. After the worship song, move into a group prayer time.

14. **CLOSING PRAYER:** *Father, we let go of any baggage from our past that we may be carrying around. We place it at the foot of the cross and expose our wounds before You. We ask You to cleanse and heal our hurts through the blood of Jesus. We receive the Father's love into every empty crevice of our hearts. We can feel good about ourselves because we have been accepted in Christ. In Jesus name, Amen.*

15. DISMISSAL
- Remind everyone about the next group meeting.
- Encourage everyone to continue to pray for each other throughout the week.
- Encourage group members to invite anybody they think will benefit from being in the group to the next meeting.
- Collect basic contact information such as phone numbers and email addresses for your group members. The Small Group Roster on page 116 of this study guide is a good place to record this information.

OUR FATHER – DAY ONE

At the heart of the Sermon on the Mount is the Lord's Prayer. Right between Jesus' words about compassion for the poor and explaining the cure for anxiety, Jesus describes prayer in a way no Rabbi had ever done before.

Jesus never intended the Lord's Prayer to morph into a religious mantra. Instead, Jesus was putting all the cards on the table by showing us how to connect with God by first seeing Him as a Father. Cultivating a spiritually healthy life and moving mountains are important to the Christian faith, but not nearly as important as how you see God relating to you.

"Our Father," the first two words of the Lord's Prayer, is where our prayer confidence begins. Why? Because it is less about how we see God and more about how God sees us. Do you realize God sees you as His? Him being "Our Father" was His idea not ours. Once we're reminded of God's desire for us, nothing can shake us and we can pray with courage and confidence.

PRAY: *Thank you, Father, for creating me as Your child. Today, I will pray with confidence; not because I am strong, but because I am Yours.*

MY DAILY JOURNAL

OUR FATHER – DAY TWO

One of the Father's primary roles is to be a good potter (Isaiah 64:8). Not only does God guide our lives, but He also shapes our lives. Our job as clay is to spin and to stay put. Prayer is how we place ourselves on the potter's wheel.

When we pray, we are giving consent to the potter to reshape us and make us more like Him. A father brings identity, provision, protection and culture to a family. But the most important thing a father brings to his children is shape. Just like a potter brings contour and purpose to the clay, our Father molds our lives in a way we can't by ourselves.

Prayer is about giving God full consent to do whatever is necessary to accomplish His will. At times, we hate the spinning or how tightly His skillful hands force the necessary changes in us, but we have to trust Him because He is first a Father who loves us.

PRAY: *Father, today, I will trust your work in my life. Though you are changing my shape, I will never fear because I know my Father loves me and has only my best interest at heart.*

MY DAILY JOURNAL

_____

_____

_____

_____

_____

_____

_____

_____

_____

_____

_____

_____

_____

_____

_____

_____

_____

_____

_____

_____

_____

_____

_____

_____

_____

OUR FATHER – DAY THREE

God is not a provision. He is a person and He wants the relationship, not just the results. Adam and Eve had to learn this the hard way. After rejecting the better tree for the lesser tree, Adam and Eve went into hiding. They traded light for shadows.

But then along comes the Father in the cool of the day (not the heat of the day) to woo them back out into the open. For a brief moment, Adam and Eve were convinced they could make it on their own – just the two of them – except they still needed the Creator's food supply.

Adam and Eve are no different than the rest of us. Our tendency is to want the help but hide from the relationship. That's why the beginning of the Lord's Prayer is so significant. When I begin my prayer time with "Our Father," it pulls me out of the shadows and back into the strength of my Father's love, presence and partnership.

PRAY: *Thank You for Your mercy, Father, and for not leaving me in hiding. It's not about my needs being met. It's about joining with You to reach this world. Thank You for loving me as a Father and for not abandoning me, even when I walk away. Your grace feels like warm daylight.*

MY DAILY JOURNAL

_____
_____
_____
_____
_____
_____
_____
_____
_____
_____
_____
_____
_____
_____
_____
_____
_____
_____
_____
_____
_____
_____
_____
_____
_____
_____

OUR FATHER – DAY FOUR

One of the most difficult challenges in life is to pray for others while we're hurting. Not only did Jesus call us to pray while wounded, He asked us to pray for those who hurt us. How? By keeping a mental picture of Jesus praying while dying on the cross so we can keep praying while carrying our cross.

What pulls us through during these times is our Father's strength. As a dad, the most crucial times I had with my kids was when they got hurt and I had to hold them in my arms while their pain dissipated. Holding them firmly is how peace was transferred from my life to theirs. A father "gifts" his kids with perspective when they get hurt. A father's love pulls them through.

There's no guarantee our day ahead will be filled with endless energy and happiness. On some days we just wake up with a heavy heart. But when we pray as Jesus taught us, we put ourselves in a position of strength – HIS strength – and our ability to pray effectively soars no matter what lies ahead.

PRAY: *Thank You, Father, for giving me Your strength when I pray, especially when my strength is low because my heart is heavy. I fully welcome Your strength into my life today.*

MY DAILY JOURNAL

_____

_____

_____

_____

_____

_____

_____

_____

_____

_____

_____

_____

_____

_____

_____

_____

_____

_____

_____

_____

_____

_____

_____

_____

OUR FATHER – DAY FIVE

Just prior to teaching the Lord's Prayer, Jesus states, "Do not be like them (hypocrites) for your Father knows what you need before you ask" (Matthew 6:8 NKJV). Most children say they spent a good chunk of their childhood vying for their dad's attention, but here we see a totally different appeal and picture. It's our Father in heaven trying to get our attention.

I remember well trying to get my dad to lay aside his busy life and spent emotions to really listen rather than just tolerating me, but it was a hit or miss proposition. Thankfully, there's nothing "hit or miss" with our heavenly Father because He knows our needs *before* we even ask.

This changes the picture entirely and releases us from trying to get His attention along with billions of other human beings. Praying with confidence starts with the realization that our Father loves us and is intimately aware of our needs. There's no need to beg because He already knows and is simply waiting to spend time with us today.

PRAY: *Father, thank You for knowing my needs even before I ask. I know You see my actual situation and the solutions that will work best.*

MY DAILY JOURNAL

_____

_____

_____

_____

_____

_____

_____

_____

_____

_____

_____

_____

_____

_____

_____

_____

_____

_____

_____

_____

_____

_____

_____

_____

OUR FATHER – DAY SIX

The fatherless heart will always be plagued by uncertainty and even despair, but a father can give a child certainty and confidence about their future. Through the stories he tells, he's able to guide the child's untested steps.

As a father places his arms around his child, there is an innate transfer of strength and peace that enables the child to think clearly and plan the future with confidence. A loving father emotionally removes any possibility of abandonment so the child can use all their energy to self-develop rather than fending off secret fears of being deserted.

Satan is always telling us we are destined to be alone. That's why a prayer life rooted in the "Father" must be our starting point. It defeats Satan's lies and eliminates the distraction of relational uncertainty. We are never alone! We belong to the Father of the universe Who daily transfers His strength to our hearts and minds.

PRAY: *Thank You, Jesus, that my heart if filled with the Father's love for me. I am not fatherless. I pray today knowing I will never be abandoned or alone. Satan is a defeated liar and I am deeply loved by my Father.*

MY DAILY JOURNAL

_____

_____

_____

_____

_____

_____

_____

_____

_____

_____

_____

_____

_____

_____

_____

_____

_____

_____

_____

_____

_____

_____

OUR FATHER – DAY SEVEN

We hear a lot today about developing a "culture of honor" in the church. The idea is that we have all come from somewhere and are now responsible to leave something behind for the next generation. In other words, no life is lived in isolation, but rather in relationship to both the past and the future.

Honor is a beautiful kingdom concept. Whether earthly or heavenly, honor (or dishonor) is often directly connected to the life of the father. Some feel they can't represent anything positive because their earthly father lived a dishonorable life. Others, however, live with purpose because the honor of their father's name was passed to them.

The Lord's Prayer should have the same effect. It creates valor and purpose in our lives because we come to understand that the honor of our heavenly Father is being lived out through our lives here on earth. We can know that we have a daily assignment that is rich with kingdom purpose.

PRAY: *Father, I represent You and the honor of Your kingdom. People will form their opinions about You based upon my life. Today, I commit to live a life for Your honor.*

MY DAILY JOURNAL

_____

_____

_____

_____

_____

_____

_____

_____

_____

_____

_____

_____

_____

_____

_____

_____

_____

_____

_____

_____

_____

_____

_____

_____

_____

_____

FORTY DAYS OF PRAYER

Session 2: YOUR KINGDOM

CHECKING IN

1. **INTRO:** If you could become the leader of any country in the world, which would it be and why? What is one thing you would do as the leader?

MEMORY VERSE

"The kingdom of God does not come with observation; nor will they say, 'See here!' or 'See there!' For indeed, the kingdom of God is within you."

Luke 17:20-21 NKJV

VIDEO

2. **WATCH:** Play the Session 2 video Scan the QR Code or go online to:

scotthaganleads.com/40-days-of-prayer

DISCUSSION QUESTIONS

3. **READ ALOUD:** Have a different person read each of the following verses or passages out loud to the group (Read all the verses and passages consecutively <u>before</u> discussing #4):
   - Psalm 24:7-10
   - Psalm 45:6
   - Psalm 104:1
   - Philippians 2:9-10
   - Revelation 1:5-6
   - Revelation 19:16

4. **ASK:** As we read those verses about the kingship of God, what stood out to you? What came to your mind?

5. **READ ALOUD:** As Scott mentioned in the video, human tendency is to be intimidated to approach a throne and stand before a powerful king.

6. **ASK:** Why is the concept of sonship *and* kingship a powerful combination? How should this transform our prayer life?

7. **READ ALOUD:** Romans 14:17.

8. **READ ALOUD:** The kingdom, or the King's domain, is inside of us. When it is fully developed it produces righteousness, peace and joy in the Holy Spirit.

9. **ASK:** Have you ever experienced an increase of righteousness, peace and joy in your life after praying?
   - If so, why do think that is?
   - In your own words, how would you describe what is happening?

10. **READ ALOUD:** The more surrendered we are to God's agenda for our life, the more we enter into the kingdom, a.k.a. the King's domain. As John the Baptist said in John 3:30, "He must increase, but I must decrease."

11. **ASK:** How can our own selfish agendas hinder our prayer life?

12. **ASK:** How can prayer help you grow in yielding to God's will?

13. **READ ALOUD:** <u>AFTER</u> we read the next question (#14) out loud, let's pause in silence for 10-15 seconds for personal reflection before answering.

14. **ASK:** Are there any areas of your life right now that you need to SURRENDER to the Lord?

PRAYER

15. **PRAYER REQUESTS:** Ask for everyone's prayer requests. Encourage everyone to briefly share their requests so you can spend more time praying for your requests than talking about them. Be sure to record them on the Small Group Prayer & Praise Report on page 119 of this study guide. Commit to pray for each other's requests every day this week. Once all the requests are gathered, move into a group prayer time.

16. **OPTIONAL:** Once you've gathered all prayer requests, play a worship song—before you pray—from a stereo or MP3 player (if your setting allows for this). If you have the song lyrics on sheets, you may pass them out. If not, encourage people to listen to the words if they're not familiar with the song. After the worship song, move into a group prayer time.

17. **CLOSING PRAYER:** *Lord, remove any intimidation or hesitancy to approach Your throne of grace in prayer. We surrender our will to Your will. Lord, bend us. Let your kingdom increase in our lives as it is in heaven.*

16. DISMISSAL

- Remind everyone about the next group meeting.
- Encourage everyone to continue to pray for each other throughout the week.
- Encourage group members to invite anybody they think will benefit from being in the group to the next meeting.

The Power of a Praying Church

YOUR KINGDOM – DAY ONE

Our perspective in prayer is radically altered when we allow Jesus to shift us from not only fatherhood, but to kingship as well. Too many believers either pray with one, or neither of these certainties. The Lord is not a powerless relative nor is He an impersonal authority. The same loving Father is also "clothed with honor and majesty" (Psalm 104:1 NKJV).

Hebrews 4:16 reminds us to "come boldly to the throne of grace" (NKJV). If we truly believe our Father sits on the throne, we can then approach Him with trust instead of timidity. We can access His power and favor while the exchange fills us with courage instead of concern.

Knowing our Father sits on the throne gives us these two profound realities, and creates a craving to pray. If prayer feels like a chore we need to re-engage in the royal relationship we have with Him. If the act of praying generates boredom, let's intentionally reconnect to our heavenly position.

PRAY: *Father, help me see You on the throne clothed with honor and majesty. I will approach You with boldness and expectation every day of my life.*

MY DAILY JOURNAL

_____

_____

_____

_____

_____

_____

_____

_____

_____

_____

_____

_____

_____

_____

_____

_____

_____

_____

_____

_____

_____

_____

YOUR KINGDOM – DAY TWO

The concept of a kingdom feels elusive and mystical. In the United States, we don't have a king with a crown, scepter or throne, so these are fuzzy concepts to the individualistic and democratic worldview. Casual individualism is not what the Bible teaches.

Even though our Father sits on His throne, our disposition shouldn't be an obsession with accomplishing our own selfish agenda. Certainly the King is our Dad but we're still under His domain and our Father's kingdom is filled with mission and purpose.

While an impersonal king will merely bark out an assignment, knowing and expressing the Father's heart is already our assignment in God's kingdom. His kingdom isn't a police state to be feared. As King and Father, His motives don't breed suspicion.

His will always fulfills. Always. So we must never lose the idea of kingship in the concept of fatherhood, nor the idea of fatherhood in the concept of kingship. When we ask for His kingdom to come, it enlists us in a greater purpose than our own self-centeredness and narcissism.

PRAY: *Father, today I open my heart to Your agenda. May Your will be done as I embrace Your kingdom purpose in my life.*

MY DAILY JOURNAL

_____

_____

_____

_____

_____

_____

_____

_____

_____

_____

_____

_____

_____

_____

_____

_____

_____

_____

_____

_____

_____

_____

_____

YOUR KINGDOM – DAY THREE

The kingdom is the King's domain. When we are living in submission and obedience to Him, we are safely positioned under the covering of the kingdom canopy. We have kingdom authority if our lives are under kingdom authority.

Our daily time in prayer allows our hearts to recalibrate to the King's domain. When the Apostle Paul prayed, he would bow his knees (Acts 20:36, Acts 21:5, Ephesians 3:14) in humility and honor to God. It was an outward expression of an inward condition. It's a reminder that the more we force our own agenda, the more we wander away from kingdom covering. Conversely, the more we yield to the Father's heart, the more authority we wield against the evil one.

In repentance, worship, and prayer we trade our power for His. We give up our futile efforts in exchange for His divine substance. Let's ask the Holy Spirit to reveal any darkness in us so we might be yielded fully and completely under our King's domain.

PRAY: *Father, I yield myself to You. Show me if there is any wicked way in me. I submit myself to Your Lordship and kingdom, in Jesus' name.*

MY DAILY JOURNAL

_____

_____

_____

_____

_____

_____

_____

_____

_____

_____

_____

_____

_____

_____

_____

_____

_____

_____

_____

_____

_____

_____

_____

_____

_____

YOUR KINGDOM – DAY FOUR

God's will must overtake our own will. This happens naturally when we are acutely aware that we are the worshiping creation and not the Creator. Our broken, fallen nature doesn't run the planet. His will does. This can be a difficult reality to accept when pride has overtaken our thinking.

When we humble ourselves and stop resisting Him, God's will becomes the final say to which we yield. Over time, God's will becomes a trusted friend rather than a frightening adversary. Eventually we realize that when God's will wins in our hearts, we win!

Prayer is the only setting that creates the proper conditions for His will to be forged in our hearts. In prayer, God invites us. He doesn't intimidate or manipulate us. Our hands are not "cuffed" under authority. Our hands are "lifted up" under authority. May His will, not ours, be done in our lives today.

PRAY: *Father, please fill me with the knowledge of Your will. Give me Your wisdom and spiritual understanding as I live in Your kingdom.*

MY DAILY JOURNAL

_____

_____

_____

_____

_____

_____

_____

_____

_____

_____

_____

_____

_____

_____

_____

_____

_____

_____

_____

_____

_____

_____

YOUR KINGDOM – DAY FIVE

Prayer is not simply a one-way monologue from us to God. Prayer is meant to be a dialogue between the Creator and His creation, but it requires us to be still in His presence at times. We must listen to God's direction for our lives because it's the pathway that conforms our will to His will and brings us peace.

The prophet Isaiah said, "Incline your ear, and come to Me; Hear and your soul shall live" (Isaiah 55:3 *NKJV*). David said, "I waited and waited and waited for God" (Psalm 40:1 *The Message*) and "Be still and know that I am God" (Psalm 46:10 NKJV*)*.

In the midst of our noisy, busy lives we can inadvertently develop noisy, busy prayers, filled with static instead of solitude. Our communion with God mimics our fast-paced, hard-charging existence. That's why we must listen to God daily because everyday is different. When we listen to God it softens our hearts that we might know His heart for us.

PRAY: *Father, I wait patiently before You today. Please soften my heart as I make time for silence. Teach my ears to listen and clearly hear Your heart.*

MY DAILY JOURNAL

_____

_____

_____

_____

_____

_____

_____

_____

_____

_____

_____

_____

_____

_____

_____

_____

_____

_____

_____

_____

_____

_____

_____

_____

_____

_____

YOUR KINGDOM – DAY SIX

How intimately acquainted do you believe God is with the details of our lives? Does He really care about everything that we will face today? Apparently so, because Jesus said in Luke 12:7, "Indeed, the very hairs of your head are all numbered" (New International Version).

God's will for our lives is very personal in nature, which runs contrary to the instincts of the fallen, human heart. We can easily feel as if our Father is a distant God Who could never be fully engaged in the minutiae of our life because He is too preoccupied with much more important things.

The truth, however, is that God is not only engrossed in the dramatic unfolding of the last days, but is also surgically attentive to the smallest areas of our lives. He desires to operate on the deeper places of our hearts and attitudes. His work is far more intricate than just taking us from "sinner" to "sinless." He also wants to move us from "foolishness" to "wisdom." He deeply desires for us to live well and finish well.

PRAY: *Father, transform me today. I want Your will, not my will, to be done. Thank You for caring about the details of my life.*

MY DAILY JOURNAL

_____

_____

_____

_____

_____

_____

_____

_____

_____

_____

_____

_____

_____

_____

_____

_____

_____

_____

_____

_____

_____

_____

_____

_____

_____

YOUR KINGDOM – DAY SEVEN

We should all have a deep spiritual hunger to see God's kingdom come right where we live. When Heaven's will is manifested in us, Jesus will be magnified through us. We must be intently praying for Heaven to touch our homes and our workplaces, our neighborhoods and the nations. Flooding Heaven with our prayers allows the Holy Spirit to flood the earth with Heaven.

For whose souls are we contending? Into what situations are we speaking blessing? What visions are we praying into reality? Prayer transforms spiritual promises from the invisible realm into visible manifestations. If faith is the evidence of things not seen, then prayer is the evidence of our faith. We pray because we have faith.

Remember, God created the world with His words (Hebrews 11:3). He started with a landscape that was without form and simply spoke it into existence. In prayer, we can speak His kingdom into the earth.

PRAY: *Father, let Your gospel reach the poor and heal the brokenhearted. Send freedom to those in captivity of sin and bring recovery of sight to the blind. Free those who are oppressed and release Your favor on our land.*

MY DAILY JOURNAL

_____

_____

_____

_____

_____

_____

_____

_____

_____

_____

_____

_____

_____

_____

_____

_____

_____

_____

_____

_____

_____

_____

Session 3: DAILY BREAD

CHECKING IN

1. **INTRO:** What is your favorite food or meal?

MEMORY VERSE

But He answered and said, "It is written, 'Man shall not live by bread alone, but by every word that proceeds from the mouth of God.'"

Matthew 4:4 NKJV

VIDEO

2. **WATCH:** Play the Session 3 video. Scan the QR Code or go online to:

scotthaganleads.com/40-days-of-prayer

DISCUSSION QUESTIONS

3. **READ ALOUD:** John 6:32-35, 48-51.

4. **ASK:** What attributes or ideas come to your mind when you think of "bread"?

5. **READ ALOUD:** John 6:35-58. (As we read this, notice all of the promises for those who come to Jesus as "the Bread of Life.")

6. **ASK:** What are some of the promises mentioned in the verses we've already read?

7. **READ ALOUD:** Jesus referenced the Old Testament story of the manna in the desert. Let's review it.

8. **READ ALOUD:** Exodus 16:2-5, 13-18.

9. **ASK:** What stands out to you?

10. **ASK:** In what ways were the children of Israel dependent on the manna?
    *   How does this speak to us about Jesus and prayer?

11. **ASK:** In your own prayer life, how have you experienced Jesus as your daily bread?

12. **ASK:** What can you do in your prayer life to grow in allowing Jesus to be your daily bread?

PRAYER

13. **PRAYER REQUESTS:** Ask for everyone's prayer requests. Be sure to record them on the Small Group Prayer and Praise Report on page 119 of this study guide. Commit to pray for each other's requests every day this week. Once all the requests are gathered, move into a group prayer time.

14. **OPTIONAL:** Once you've gathered all prayer requests, play a worship song—before you pray—from a stereo or MP3 player (if your setting allows for this). After the worship song, move into a group prayer time.

15. **CLOSING PRAYER:** *Lord Jesus, give our souls the daily bread of Your life. We ask for Your presence to touch our spirits. We ask for Your love to touch our hearts. And we receive Your provision for all of our needs, in Jesus' name. Amen.*

11. **DISMISSAL**
- Remind everyone about the next group meeting.
- Encourage everyone to continue to pray for each other throughout the week.

DAILY BREAD – DAY ONE

At the start of a new week, it can be very tempting, even seemingly prudent, to take a long view of the days ahead. But all of the thinking, planning, arranging and even anticipating of conflicts can make us exhausted long before we even get out of bed.

We have to remember that the non-negotiable first step, at the start of anything new, must be prayer. Whether it's a new job, relationship, purchase or even just a new day, how we begin will go a long way toward determining the success of our efforts. Yes, we all have long-term needs, but worrying about tomorrow accomplishes nothing for today.

It all comes down to our immediate focus. Rather than allowing what's facing us this week to overwhelm our senses, let's choose to focus on what's in front of us today. As we seek God for His blessing and divine direction, we must allow Jesus' prayer in Matthew 6:11 to be our guide, "Give us today the food we need … " (NLT).

PRAY: *Father, I begin today completely confident You have already made provision for everything I will need. Help me leave my worries about tomorrow for another day.*

MY DAILY JOURNAL

_____

_____

_____

_____

_____

_____

_____

_____

_____

_____

_____

_____

_____

_____

_____

_____

_____

_____

_____

_____

_____

_____

DAILY BREAD – DAY TWO

In the frantic pace of an average day, we can be easily consumed with the overwhelming weight of responsibility. We are spouses, parents, employers, employees, students, friends, teammates, as well as a plethora of other roles. Trying to balance them all can seem a completely unachievable task, especially when our emotional energy is depleted.

According to the U.S. Labor Department, over 2 million Americans quit their jobs every month. Why? Although reasons include not getting along with a boss or a lack of empowerment, the primary reason seems to be a lack of personal recognition. In other words, we give it our best but no one seems to notice or care.

The secret to making it through today is not what we do, but to remember for Whom we're doing it. We simply won't get what we need from the approval of others. Our sense of self-worth comes only from a daily relationship with our heavenly Father. He is the only One who can give us what we need for today.

PRAY: *Father, help me today to find my sense of value not in what I accomplish but in who I am in You. I choose Your approval as my "food" for today.*

MY DAILY JOURNAL

_____

_____

_____

_____

_____

_____

_____

_____

_____

_____

_____

_____

_____

_____

_____

_____

_____

_____

_____

_____

_____

_____

DAILY BREAD – DAY THREE

For six days every week for 40 years it never changed. The dreariness of the mundane had long past settled into the consciousness of a culture. The Israelites had been instructed to collect the "manna" God had faithfully provided every morning. It was literally their food for the day. The routine became second nature. It was a morning ritual they would perform thousands of times without a second thought as to the divine source of their supernatural provision.

Scripture records they became so focused on a future filled with "milk and honey" that they devalued the daily miracle right before their eyes. They were so intent on gaining something else they weren't grateful for what they had already been given.

When we overlook or even trivialize the "appetizer" today, we jeopardize the "main course" tomorrow. We must trust that our all-knowing Father delights in taking care of us now, all the while preparing what we will need later.

PRAY: *Father, I trust You to provide for me exactly what I need for today; nothing more and nothing less. Thank You for so faithfully providing for me.*

MY DAILY JOURNAL

_____

_____

_____

_____

_____

_____

_____

_____

_____

_____

_____

_____

_____

_____

_____

_____

_____

_____

_____

_____

_____

_____

_____

DAILY BREAD – DAY FOUR

We've all experienced something completely unanticipated that interrupts the flow of our day. Out of nowhere comes a curve ball, an unexpected twist that catches us completely off guard. If we're not spiritually prepared we can quickly become frustrated and even emotionally derailed. We wonder in confusion, "What in the world just happened?"

Though life often takes us by surprise, believers find great comfort in knowing our loving Father sees the end from the beginning. Nothing has or ever will challenge His confidence. He's still firmly seated on His throne.

That's why it's absolutely crucial to begin each morning on our knees because only God knows exactly what lies ahead. His mercies are new every morning (Lamentations 3:22-23) but His provision is always unique to the day at hand. He gives us exactly what we need. In fact, the strength for today is already waiting for us to receive it.

PRAY: *Father, help me to walk in Your strength today. No matter what happens, You've given me exactly what I need.*

MY DAILY JOURNAL

_____

_____

_____

_____

_____

_____

_____

_____

_____

_____

_____

_____

_____

_____

_____

_____

_____

_____

_____

_____

_____

_____

_____

_____

DAILY BREAD – DAY FIVE

Before Jesus walked on the earth, the Israelites faced legitimate limitations in having a personal relationship with God. The temple veil had not yet been torn, the Holy Spirit had not yet been sent and all the Scriptures had not yet been written.

Instead, they participated in annual feasts. Some were required as a sacrifice while others were forms of celebration. At some point, weekly worship at the Temple became commonplace, increasing the commitment to every seven days. But after Jesus ascended to Heaven we see the disciples praying daily at the temple. It became spiritually customary— a welcomed devotional habit. The Bible clearly instructs us today to pray without ceasing (1 Thessalonians 5:17 NKJV), to seek God's face continually.

Thankfully, we don't worship a "once a year" or even a "once a week" deity. We have a "daily" God Who desperately wants to be involved in our lives without casual interruption. Let's seek His face today and not wait until church this weekend.

PRAY: *Father, help me cultivate a burning desire to seek You every day; not later, but right now. Daily time with You is key to being victorious in my life.*

MY DAILY JOURNAL

_____

_____

_____

_____

_____

_____

_____

_____

_____

_____

_____

_____

_____

_____

_____

_____

_____

_____

_____

_____

_____

_____

_____

_____

DAILY BREAD – DAY SIX

Everywhere we look we're surrounded by people who seem to have more than we do. Larger salaries, bigger homes, nicer cars, better clothes, less dysfunctional families ... and the list continues. Why are we so easily enamored with what we don't have instead of what we've already been given? Is it really that we're not grateful for what we possess, or is it rather an uncontrollable, irrational drive to prove our internal value by the external value of our net worth?

Jesus modeled for us asking only for our daily bread, allowing God alone to worry about all of our tomorrows. In fact, could it be that our Father intentionally creates conditions that teach us to rely on Him instead of ourselves? Does He actually delight in helping us grow our faith by placing us in specific situations where we simply can't be our own solution?

Proverbs 30:8 declares, "Give me neither poverty nor riches! Give me just enough to satisfy my needs" (NLT). May it be that we, His people, accept His provision for today with a grateful heart.

PRAY: *Father, I realize You have given me everything I need for today. I am truly thankful.*

MY DAILY JOURNAL

_____

_____

_____

_____

_____

_____

_____

_____

_____

_____

_____

_____

_____

_____

_____

_____

_____

_____

_____

_____

_____

_____

_____

_____

_____

DAILY BREAD – DAY SEVEN

There is something incredible that happens in the lives of believers when we make a daily commitment to prayer. It kindles a spiritual fire that is an unquenchable fuel for our journey. It's a power source our enemy can't ever extinguish, regardless of how hard he may try.

In the Old Testament, the Levitical priests were instructed to carefully maintain the sacrificial fire so that the altar's flame never died. "The fire on the altar must be kept burning; it must never go out. Each morning ... add fresh wood to the fire ..." (Leviticus 6:12 NLT).

What a profound principle to infuse into our daily lives! Every single morning we must intentionally add fresh "wood" to the fire within our spirit, seeking God's presence as well as guidance to recognize His provision. Our daily bread is always available when we choose to spend those quiet, life-refreshing moments with Him.

PRAY: *Father, today I choose to intentionally put fresh wood on the altar of my heart. I yield to Your will, trusting You to provide exactly what I need and to lead me wherever I should go.*

MY DAILY JOURNAL

_____

_____

_____

_____

_____

_____

_____

_____

_____

_____

_____

_____

_____

_____

_____

_____

_____

_____

_____

_____

_____

_____

_____

Session 4: FORGIVENESS

CHECKING IN

1. **INTRO:** What do you value most in your relationships with other people?

MEMORY VERSE

And be kind to one another, tenderhearted, forgiving one another, even as God in Christ forgave you.
                                    Ephesians 4:32 NKJV

VIDEO

2. **WATCH:** Play the Session 4 video. Scan the QR Code or go online to:

scotthaganleads.com/40-days-of-prayer

DISCUSSION QUESTIONS

3. **READ ALOUD:** In the video, Scott said forgiveness can't be slow and selective.

4. **ASK:** How does a consistent prayer life strengthen our spiritual muscles to forgive quickly and completely?

5. **ASK:** Why does the Lord's Prayer make us consistently revisit the issue of total forgiveness?

6. **ASK:** In your own words, why and how does bitterness and resentment hinder our prayers?

7. **READ ALOUD:** Psalm 139:23-24.

8. **READ ALOUD:** To walk in forgiveness, we need to regularly ask the Holy Spirit to search our hearts and reveal any hidden resentment or bitterness.

9. **ASK:** What type of disposition or frame of mind must we exercise in prayer to allow the Holy Spirit to reveal hidden bondages in our hearts?
    *   How is that contrary to a busy, noisy lifestyle?

10. **ASK:** How is it difficult for you to walk in total forgiveness? Be as specific as possible.

11. **PRAYER EXERCISE:** In a brief prayer over the group, ask the Holy Spirit to search each person's heart and reveal any areas of unforgiveness. Pause and sit in silence for 30 seconds to listen and reflect. After the 30 seconds of silence, lead the group in the following prayer. Read one short phrase at a time and have them repeat it after you:

    Lord Jesus, I forgive those who have trespassed against me. I release them from having to make amends with me. I declare to You and myself that they owe me nothing because they are forgiven. Heal my heart from the poison of hurt and bitterness. Create in me a clean heart and give me the power to forgive, just as You have forgiven me. In Jesus' name. Amen.

PRAYER

12. **OPTIONAL:** Listen to a worship song as a group before gathering prayer requests.

13. **PRAYER REQUESTS:** Subgroup by gender or in smaller groups of 3-4 people. Ask everyone to share his or her prayer requests in the smaller groups. Once the requests are gathered, the subgroups should pray for one another. After the meeting, be sure to record prayer requests on the Small Group Prayer and Praise Report on page 119 of this study guide. Commit to pray for each other's requests every day this week.

14. **DISMISSAL**
- Remind everyone about the next group meeting.
- Encourage everyone to continue to pray for each other throughout the week.

FORGIVENESS – DAY ONE

Spiritual maturity is not measured by our inability to offend others, but by our inability to be offended by others. In the Lord's Prayer, which contains the daily components of the Christian life, it's powerfully revealing that forgiveness is included.

Most people think of forgiveness in terms of their own salvation, or a small number of life events that required them "to forgive somebody" of something "really big." But the Lord's Prayer clearly indicates that forgiveness is more daily than occasional. It reminds us of when Jesus blew apart Peter's "forgiveness math" in Matthew 18:21-22 (NLT). Peter asked, "Lord, how often should I forgive someone who sins against me? Seven times?" Jesus' response? "No, not seven times ... seventy times seven" (490 times).

Jesus taught us that forgiveness is continual and not just a random act. We must begin our day ready to forgive, so any offense, even painful ones, shouldn't catch us off guard.

PRAY: *Lord, fill my life today with Your love and Your power to forgive everyone of everything. No matter how many times someone wrongs me, I completely release them just as You completely released me of my sins.*

MY DAILY JOURNAL

_____

_____

_____

_____

_____

_____

_____

_____

_____

_____

_____

_____

_____

_____

_____

_____

_____

_____

_____

_____

_____

_____

_____

_____

FORGIVENESS – DAY TWO

One of the most important aspects of total forgiveness is speed. How fast can you do it? Biblical forgiveness doesn't have a cooling off period in which the wounded or offended assesses the damage before declaring someone free.

People often confuse forgiveness with trust, but they are very different. Trust grows with time, but forgiveness happens instantly. As Jesus was dying on the cross with blood flowing down His face, forgiveness flowed as well. "Father, forgive them, for they do not know what they do" (Luke 23:34 NKJV).

Jesus didn't wait for the blood to dry, scab and scar so He could look in the mirror, calculate the long-term effects of their actions and then measure His forgiveness accordingly. No, Jesus forgave immediately and thoroughly. It's the only kind of forgiveness the Bible teaches. That's why it was so central to the "Lord's Prayer". Is it hard? Yes! Holding on to pain is an easier choice, but the long-term consequences are deadly.

PRAY: *Lord, help me today to quickly forgive those who hurt me, whether it's on accident or on purpose. Help me to trust You quickly, not letting time pass, jeopardizing my heart.*

MY DAILY JOURNAL

_____

_____

_____

_____

_____

_____

_____

_____

_____

_____

_____

_____

_____

_____

_____

_____

_____

_____

_____

_____

_____

_____

FORGIVENESS – DAY THREE

Biblical forgiveness isn't selective. It's comprehensive. In other words, Jesus wants us to always forgive everyone of everything. The moment we classify our wounds and put them into separate categories we are falling into Satan's trap.

When we trust God, we attract even more of His grace. I Peter 5:5 says that God "resists the proud, but gives grace to the humble" (NKJV). Having our hearts softened, even toward a betrayer, is not something we're naturally born to do. It's incredibly difficult and requires God's love working in us. Showing genuine humility is how we access the full power of God in our lives. When it's there, we can accomplish amazing things. We can even forgive everyone of everything.

Asking God to forgive us of our debts and forgiving others of their debts against us are not and cannot be two separate actions. According to Jesus' teaching through the Lord's Prayer, they are always one and the same.

PRAY: *Father, Your power inside me gives me the strength to forgive everyone of everything. Keep me from being selective in whom and how I forgive, but instead to forgive the way Jesus did.*

MY DAILY JOURNAL

FORGIVENESS – DAY FOUR

Being free means I've "let go" of others' actions that have negatively distracted or destroyed me emotionally. We may always have the memory, but we can be free from how it triggers anxiety or thoughts of retribution.

Unforgiveness is a pipeline that constantly pumps darkness into our hearts. Perhaps most difficult are the emotions that travel with our unforgiving attitudes that can feel like an independent system working inside our minds. The idea that we have no control of our feelings – that they just seem to march to their own drumbeat – is far from reality!

In Scripture, the "heart" is the seat of our emotional well-being. Forgiveness dismantles the toxic pipeline and restores to us the control of our heart. When we control our hearts, we also control our emotions. Though there are rare occasions where medical imbalances exist, the majority of emotional issues are spiritual in nature. The heart must be in proper order, and the Lord's Prayer shows it's possible with diligent daily effort.

PRAY: *Father, I realize a heart that is spiritually free from unforgiveness is a heart that is also emotionally free. Help me let go of offenses so I can be free from the enemy's "trigger points" that try to pull me backward.*

MY DAILY JOURNAL

_____

_____

_____

_____

_____

_____

_____

_____

_____

_____

_____

_____

_____

_____

_____

_____

_____

_____

_____

_____

_____

_____

_____

_____

_____

_____

FORGIVENESS – DAY FIVE

Unforgiveness is Satan's way of stealing the momentum from our lives. Satan doesn't want us to grow. He wants us to squander away our days and resources. The battle is great! That's why some of the greatest worshippers of Jesus still struggle to find ways of justifying their unforgiving attitudes and actions. In fact, next to pride, unforgiveness is the primary way Satan keeps a person spiritually ordinary.

A life of total forgiveness is hard, but not impossible. The stakes are high because of the reward for us and the generation to follow are both great. What are we saying? This is not a small issue. It's the primary issue of life!

That's why it's included in the Lord's Prayer. We must take this journey seriously. It can't just be placed on the "to do" list of things to get to later. From the very beginning of our day we must choose a life of total forgiveness ... and then choose it again tomorrow.

PRAY: *Lord, today I make spiritual freedom my top priority. I stand firmly against Satan's attacks to steal my resources and time by distracting me through thoughts of unforgiveness.*

MY DAILY JOURNAL

_____

_____

_____

_____

_____

_____

_____

_____

_____

_____

_____

_____

_____

_____

_____

_____

_____

_____

_____

_____

_____

_____

FORGIVENESS – DAY SIX

Do you know it's not enough to just forgive your enemy? Jesus tells us that we must also bless them! Undoubtedly, the kingdom of heaven is vastly different than the kingdom of man. When unforgiveness is removed from the heart, it leaves a vacuum that must be filled by new emotions, behaviors and actions that are kingdom centered.

Jesus promised that He would give us the power to bless our enemies. It's not impossible! It may begin with something as simple as speaking differently. Instead of talking negatively about the person who wronged us, we remain silent or simply say, with a smile, that the situation is fully resolved.

When we stop talking about "the situation," the people around us will stop talking about it as well. Then, by choosing to bless our enemies, it cements our forgiveness and becomes one of the most important parts of our testimony as we move forward in kingdom authority.

Have you moved from forgiveness to blessing your enemy?

PRAY: *Lord, choosing to bless my enemies as part of a lifestyle of forgiveness is extremely difficult to do and one of the most important parts of my testimony. Help me to forgive and bless those who have offended me.*

MY DAILY JOURNAL

_____

_____

_____

_____

_____

_____

_____

_____

_____

_____

_____

_____

_____

_____

_____

_____

_____

_____

_____

_____

_____

_____

_____

_____

_____

FORGIVENESS – DAY SEVEN

Receiving personal forgiveness is often harder to understand than the idea of giving forgiveness away to someone else. You would think that being forgiven is a no brainer, but it can be difficult to fathom how God can release us from the "really big sins" we have committed.

Joseph was betrayed by his brothers. 20 years later, he forgave and welcomed them into his home. They were stunned he didn't kill them for what they had done. After another 17 years, their father Jacob finally passed away. The brothers became terrified that Joseph would finally, after 37 years, take his revenge. All Joseph could do was what he had been doing all along. He continued to speak kindly to them and provide for them.

It's the same for us; it's hard sometimes to truly believe we've been forgiven of everything we've ever done – the "big" things, the "secret things" – but we have! Now, we must do the same for others.

PRAY: *Father, thank You for forgiving me of everything I have ever done. Now empower me to follow in Your footsteps by forgiving others of everything they have done to me.*

MY DAILY JOURNAL

_____

_____

_____

_____

_____

_____

_____

_____

_____

_____

_____

_____

_____

_____

_____

_____

_____

_____

_____

_____

_____

_____

_____

Session 5: TEMPTATION

CHECKING IN

1. **INTRO:** If you could attempt absolutely anything with guaranteed success, what would it be and why?

MEMORY VERSE

No temptation has overtaken you except such as is common to man; but God is faithful, who will not allow you to be tempted beyond what you are able, but with the temptation will also make the way of escape, that you may be able to bear it.

1 Corinthians 10:13 NKJV

VIDEO

2. **WATCH:** Play the Session 5 video. Scan the QR Code or go online to:

scotthaganleads.com/40-days-of-prayer

DISCUSSION QUESTIONS

3. **READ ALOUD:** James 1:14-15.

4. **READ ALOUD:** James says the starting point of temptation is our own desires.

5. **ASK:** What stands out to you in that passage in regard to temptation?

6. **READ ALOUD:** Matthew 26:36-46.

7. **READ ALOUD:** This passage tells about one of Jesus' greatest trials and temptations.

8. **EXERCISE:** Write down the verse numbers that use the words "prayer," "pray" or "prayed."

9. **SHARE:** Share the verses that use the words "prayer," "pray" or "prayed."

10. **ASK:** How does seeing the importance of prayer in Jesus' greatest trial speak to you?

11. **ASK:** What trials and temptations *have* you faced or *are* you facing in your life?

12. **ASK:** How does consistent prayer empower you to resist temptation?

13. **ASK:** What Christ-like character qualities can you develop by defeating the most common temptations you face?

PRAYER

14. **PRAYER REQUESTS:** Ask for everyone's prayer requests. Be sure to record them on the Small Group Prayer and Praise Report on page 119 of this study guide. Commit to pray for each other's requests every day this week. Once all the requests are gathered, move into a group prayer time.

15. **OPTIONAL:** Once you've gathered all prayer requests, play a worship song—before you pray—from a stereo or MP3 player (if your setting allows for this). After the worship song,

move into a group prayer time.

16. **CLOSING PRAYER:** *Lord Jesus, help us experience intimacy with You through prayer. Let our affection for You be greater than the lust of this world. Sharpen our discernment so we can follow You and practice the truth in freedom. We receive Your power to walk in obedience. In Jesus' name. Amen.*

17. **DISMISSAL**
    - Remind everyone about the next group meeting.
    - Encourage everyone to continue to pray for each other throughout the week.

TEMPTATION – DAY ONE

Temptation is an undeniable fact of life. There's no avoiding it or getting around it. No matter our age or stage, we must constantly be on guard for the unguarded areas in our lives that leave us vulnerable to spiritual attack. Temptation may have its origin in the weakness of our flesh but it only comes to fruition with the permission of our will.

That's why the Apostle Paul warns us to "Stay away from every kind of evil" and admonished Timothy to "Run from anything that stimulates youthful lusts" (1 Thessalonians 5:22, 2 Timothy 2:22 NLT). Jesus clearly said we are "in" this world and we would "have trouble" (John 16:33 NIV). This is why He didn't instruct us to pray that we wouldn't be tempted but rather that we would possess the supernatural strength to withstand it.

So let us live with the intention of honoring God not by preventing temptation, but by allowing the Holy Spirit to enable us to always stand strong.

PRAY: *Father, I know that being tempted is unavoidable in this life, so today I acknowledge my desperate need for Your strength to not yield when temptation occurs.*

MY DAILY JOURNAL

_____

_____

_____

_____

_____

_____

_____

_____

_____

_____

_____

_____

_____

_____

_____

_____

_____

_____

_____

_____

_____

_____

TEMPTATION – DAY TWO

Though we may have been taught to believe otherwise, temptation isn't a sin. In fact, even Jesus Himself, who lived His life on this earth perfectly, without a single mistake, was tempted in EVERY way humanly possible (Hebrews 4:15). It's reassuring to know there isn't a single temptation we will face that Jesus didn't personally have to zealously resist as well.

One of our enemy's greatest weapons is to make us feel spiritually defeated and emotionally isolated because we're experiencing temptation. But rather than allowing our energy to be drained, we must remember the priceless instruction we read in James 4:7, "Humble yourselves before God. Resist the devil, and he will flee from you" (NLT).

The strength of our ability to resist the devil is directly tied to the depth of humility we possess. Arrogant people are more susceptible to temptation, but a humble spirit is a strong defense against sin. Jesus was the perfect example of humility, and His standard must be our daily goal.

PRAY: *Father, help me choose humility over arrogance. I know it's my best weapon against the temptation I will undoubtedly face today.*

MY DAILY JOURNAL

_____

_____

_____

_____

_____

_____

_____

_____

_____

_____

_____

_____

_____

_____

_____

_____

_____

_____

_____

_____

_____

_____

_____

_____

TEMPTATION – DAY THREE

We've acknowledged that all believers will experience temptation. It's disappointing but true. What's important, however, is to be cognizant of the difference between being tempted and being spiritually tried. While the Bible is explicit that God never tempts us (James 1:13), He certainly will bring trials our way that allow us opportunities for growth. "Fire tests the purity of silver and gold, but the LORD tests the heart" (Proverbs 17:3 NLT).

It's critical that we carefully discern whether we are experiencing a temptation or a trial. One is deviously designed for our destruction while the other is divinely inspired for our benefit. A temptation must be firmly resisted but a trial must be embraced with our whole heart.

Is that possible? Yes, by following Jesus' example! In a trial, He drew on God's strength through prayer but, when tempted, He quoted Scripture directly to the Tempter. When we talk directly to our temptations and pray our way through trials, we'll come through the fire as pure gold.

PRAY: *Father, give me the wisdom to discern between trials and temptations, having the courage to persevere and the strength to stand.*

MY DAILY JOURNAL

_____

_____

_____

_____

_____

_____

_____

_____

_____

_____

_____

_____

_____

_____

_____

_____

_____

_____

_____

_____

_____

_____

TEMPTATION – DAY FOUR

When we carefully read the Lord's Prayer, we're clearly reminded of our desperate need for God's daily intervention in our lives. Simply stated, we are incomplete and incapable by ourselves. We try. We fail. We become discouraged. We're tempted to give up.

That's why Jesus modeled for us how to ask for God's help in resisting the all-encompassing reach of temptation. So, rather than constantly wishing God wouldn't allow temptation to enter our lives in the first place, we must instead focus on His ability to completely deliver us. We can find comfort knowing He always limits our temptations to the current level of our spiritual growth.

Consider the words of Paul in 1 Corinthians 10:13: "God is faithful. He will not allow the temptation to be more than you can stand. When you are tempted, He will show you a way out so that you can endure" (NLT). The way out comes from God, but the decision to leave is ours.

PRAY: *Father, thank You for making a way out of the temptation I'm currently facing, and giving me unwavering strength as I make the decision to leave it behind.*

MY DAILY JOURNAL

_____

_____

_____

_____

_____

_____

_____

_____

_____

_____

_____

_____

_____

_____

_____

_____

_____

_____

_____

_____

_____

_____

_____

_____

_____

TEMPTATION – DAY FIVE

As we build our spiritual muscle to resist the plans of our crafty enemy, it's crucial we understand the symbiotic relationship between internal and external temptation. External comes from a source outside of ourselves while internal is a product of our own mental processes and the thoughts we entertain. Each affects the other.

When Potiphar's wife attempted to seduce Joseph, it was an external force acting in direct opposition to an internal conviction (Genesis 39:7-10). Even though the consequences would prove devastating in the short-term, his commitment to living a life above reproach resulted not only in his long-term triumph, but also in the preservation of his family and even an entire nation.

When external temptation occurs, we must always keep an eternal view in mind. Trouble today just sets us up for victory later, but the outcome is up to us. Joseph said, "...you meant evil against me, but God meant it for good in order to bring about this present result" (Genesis 50:20 New American Standard Bible). Resisting temptation is always worth the effort and well worth the wait.

PRAY: *Father, help me resist the external forces vying for my attention. I will wait for Your best.*

MY DAILY JOURNAL

_____

_____

_____

_____

_____

_____

_____

_____

_____

_____

_____

_____

_____

_____

_____

_____

_____

_____

_____

_____

_____

_____

_____

_____

_____

TEMPTATION – DAY SIX

The greatest attacks of temptation aren't from outside the fortress of our mental walls. Though dangerous external forces are constantly at work against us, desiring our very soul, the reality is that the conflict lurking within us can prove far more deadly. In fact, we can lose even before we begin.

How? Because what we think goes a long way toward determining what we do. The idea that we can intentionally or unintentionally "dwell" on something in our heart and mind without it subtly working its way into our subconscious desires is simply absurd. Every action, both good and bad, has its beginnings as a simple thought.

The secret isn't found in avoiding all alluring thoughts or enticing situations. That would be a completely impossible task. Rather, it's quickly recognizing wrong thoughts as they occur, and immediately subjecting them to the overcoming power of the Holy Spirit (2 Corinthians 10:5). Temptation requires moral darkness to thrive. It can't flourish in spiritual light.

PRAY: *Father, help me quickly recognize when temptation is attempting to enter my thought life. I fully submit my heart and mind to You today.*

MY DAILY JOURNAL

TEMPTATION – DAY SEVEN

As we've stated, temptation is something we'll endure for the rest of our natural lives. It's a deadly weapon in our enemy's arsenal that he uses to incessantly test our resolve, hoping that today is the day we'll finally yield. Maybe today is the day we'll fall prey to his evil scheme.

To be sure, we have all succumbed to the power of temptation, and, most likely, we will again in the future. Does this mean it's a hopeless battle? Are we destined to fight and resist only to eventually lose the war anyway? With the Holy Spirit's help, the answer is a resounding, "No!"

But we can't just pray and hope that our ability to resist temptation supernaturally increases. We must master our ability to use the tools God has given us, not to survive but to thrive! Paul gave us these priceless words in Philippians 4:8: "Fix your thoughts on what is true, honorable, right, pure, lovely and admirable ... things that are excellent and worthy of praise" (NLT). So how do we take control of our thought life? By choosing to meditate on those things God says are valuable and worthy.

PRAY: *Father, help me fix my thoughts. Temptation may come, but it will not stay, in Jesus' name.*

MY DAILY JOURNAL

_____

_____

_____

_____

_____

_____

_____

_____

_____

_____

_____

_____

_____

_____

_____

_____

_____

_____

_____

_____

_____

_____

_____

_____

_____

_____

Session 6: DELIVER US

CHECKING IN

1. **INTRO:** Can you think of a moment in your life when you felt victorious (for example, at school, playing sports, in your career, in your personal life)?

MEMORY VERSE

For He has rescued us from the dominion of darkness and brought us into the kingdom of the Son He loves.
Colossians 1:13 NIV

VIDEO

2. **WATCH:** Play the Session 6 video. Scan the QR Code or go online to:

scotthaganleads.com/40-days-of-prayer

DISCUSSION QUESTIONS

3. **READ ALOUD:** Ephesians 6:12.

4. **ASK:** Why is it valuable to discover that our battle is *not* against flesh and blood?
   - How does that help us?

5. **READ ALOUD:** Colossians 2:15.

6. **ASK:** How does being aware of Christ's authority and victory transform us?

7. **ASK:** Is there a specific spiritual battle you're in the midst of now?
   - How can prayer make a difference in your battle?

8. **ASK:** What feelings and emotions does the enemy use to distract us from prayer?
   - How are those triggered in your own life at times?

9. **READ ALOUD:** Prayer is an offensive weapon in spiritual warfare.

10. **ASK:** When you look at your life, are you being as offensive to the enemy, in prayer, as you could be?
    - How could you go on the offense more?
    - What would that look like?

PRAYER

11. **PRAYER REQUESTS:** Ask for everyone's prayer requests. Be sure to record them on the Small Group Prayer and Praise Report on page119 of this study guide. Commit to pray for each other's requests every day this week. Once all the requests are gathered, move into a group prayer time.

12. **OPTIONAL:** Once you've gathered all prayer requests, play a worship song—before you pray—from a stereo or MP3 player (if your setting allows for this). After the worship song, move into a group prayer time.

13. **CLOSING PRAYER:** *Lord Jesus, give us a spirit of wisdom and revelation that we may know Your power toward us who believe. Reveal to us the working of Your power, which You demonstrated in the resurrection. Amen.*

14. DISMISSAL

- Remind everyone about the next group meeting.
- Encourage everyone to continue to pray for each other throughout the week.

DELIVER US – DAY ONE

Today, we are in a battle. This battle will come in many different forms. We may run into a person bringing a false accusation against us. It might be a two-faced co-worker or a money-laundering business partner. Our battle, however, is actually not with any of these people.

Ephesians 6:12 says, "We are not fighting against flesh-and-blood enemies, but against evil rulers and authorities of the unseen world, against mighty powers in this dark world, and against evil spirits in the heavenly places" (NLT). Our battle is with the invisible enemy of our soul, Satan. Jesus called him a thief who comes only to "steal, and to kill, and to destroy" (John 10:10 NKJV).

Our foe can only be engaged through the power of Christ-centered prayer. What are we facing today that we haven't covered yet in prayer? We must surrender these situations to the Lord "for the battle is not yours, but God's" (2 Chronicles 20:15 NLT).

PRAY: *Father, today, I place every relationship and situation into Your hands. In my life, I claim Your power and victory over Satan, and trust You to deliver me from the evil one.*

MY DAILY JOURNAL

_____
_____
_____
_____
_____
_____
_____
_____
_____
_____
_____
_____
_____
_____
_____
_____
_____
_____
_____
_____
_____
_____
_____
_____
_____

DELIVER US – DAY TWO

Our ability to pray and ask Jesus to "deliver us from evil" is rooted in the reality of Jesus' upper hand in the spiritual realm. He said, "All authority has been given to Me in heaven and on earth" (Matthew 28:18 NKJV). There's not a square inch of heaven or earth that isn't under the jurisdiction of the name of Jesus Christ (Psalm 24:1).

When we pray with sincere hearts in the name of Jesus, we are standing in His authority, not ours. Our name holds no spiritual power, but God has "given Him the name which is above every name, that at the name of Jesus every knee should bow ... that every tongue should confess that Jesus Christ is Lord" (Philippians 2:9-11 NKJV).

When Jesus returns, we know He will have a name visibly written on Him: "King of Kings and Lord of Lords" (Revelation 19:16 NKJV). Nothing can defeat him! No name is more powerful! There is absolute power to deliver in Jesus name!

PRAY: *Father, You are greater than anything I will face. Thank You for the power in Jesus' name that causes me to be an overcomer. I will walk in His authority today.*

MY DAILY JOURNAL

_____

_____

_____

_____

_____

_____

_____

_____

_____

_____

_____

_____

_____

_____

_____

_____

_____

_____

_____

_____

_____

_____

_____

DELIVER US – DAY THREE

Jesus has utterly defeated the evil one on our behalf. Colossians 2:14-15 says, "He canceled the record of the charges against us and took it away by nailing it to the cross. In this way, he disarmed the spiritual rulers and authorities. He shamed them publicly by His victory over them on the cross" (NLT).

Through Christ's death on the cross, there was a simultaneous "search and seizure" of Satan's power. How do we know? Because the word "disarmed" means that not only were Satan's weapons removed, but he was also left humiliated and exposed. He was rendered powerless and defeated.

The public shaming mentioned in this passage is an intentional reference to the triumphal procession in Roman times (see also 2 Corinthians 2:14). When a Roman general had won a notable victory, he was allowed to march his victorious armies through the streets of Rome. Behind them followed the kings, leaders and people he had defeated. This shows us that Satan has been clearly branded as Jesus' defeated foe.

PRAY: *Father, thank You for the victory of the cross in my life that has delivered me from the evil one. Thank You for leading me daily in the processional triumph of Christ.*

MY DAILY JOURNAL

_____

_____

_____

_____

_____

_____

_____

_____

_____

_____

_____

_____

_____

_____

_____

_____

_____

_____

_____

_____

_____

_____

_____

_____

DELIVER US – DAY FOUR

Our enemy has been utterly defeated. However, he has not yet been destroyed. Until Jesus returns, we're living in the space between evil being defeated at the cross and its final destruction in the lake of fire (Revelation 20:10).

As children of God, we have already been delivered. Colossians 1:13 declares over us, "For He rescued us from the domain of darkness, and transferred us to the kingdom of His beloved Son" (NASB). Jesus is the hero of our soul, having personally pulled us from the clutches of the evil one.

We can find spiritual rest in having been rescued. However, even though our defeated enemy no longer has authority over us, we still live in a fallen world. So when he tries to taunt us, we just remind him that he can't touch us. We pray from our position of victory and faith in Christ because the domain of darkness can only be assaulted from the King's domain.

PRAY: *Father, help me to be completely anchored in Your gift of salvation. Open the eyes of my heart to see myself free from darkness as I live under the banner of Your love. I know the enemy can't touch me because I am truly free in Christ.*

MY DAILY JOURNAL

DELIVER US – DAY FIVE

In a military battle, the high ground is the advantageous position. It gives its occupier the greatest arc of observation—an unobstructed line of fire—and allows for a greater range of communications. It's also far easier to move downhill than uphill.

In Ephesians 1:20-21, Paul says that God raised Jesus "from the dead and seated Him at His right hand in the heavenly places, far above all principality and power and might and dominion, and every name that is named, not only in this age but also in that which is to come" (NKJV). Jesus has the ultimate high ground!

Paul goes on to say that God "raised us up together and made us sit together in the heavenly places in Christ Jesus" (Ephesians 2:6 NKJV). In Christ, we share in His high ground, which is why it's so critical to pray according to our heavenly position rather than our external circumstances.

PRAY: *Father, thank You for lifting me above the powers of evil. I ask You to lift my mind, will and emotions above every challenge in my life today, in Jesus' name.*

MY DAILY JOURNAL

_____

_____

_____

_____

_____

_____

_____

_____

_____

_____

_____

_____

_____

_____

_____

_____

_____

_____

_____

_____

_____

_____

_____

_____

DELIVER US – DAY SIX

Matthew 16:19 says, "I will give you the keys of the kingdom of heaven; and whatever you bind on earth shall have been bound in heaven, and whatever you loose on earth shall have been loosed in heaven" (NASB). Notice the past tense: "shall have been." This confirms for us that the battle in Heaven has already been decided.

In Heaven, all the powers of evil have already been bound. Hopelessness, doubt and depression don't exist before God's throne. So, as we bind the powers of darkness that are attempting to hold us back, we are merely releasing on earth what has already been accomplished in Heaven.

Scripture tells us that Heaven is filled with peace, love, joy and righteousness. As we pray the principles of the Lord's Prayer, it looses these heavenly realities not only to earth but also to our soul. We can live knowing that the enemy has been bound and our victory is complete.

PRAY: *Father, thank You for the victory that has been won in heaven. In Jesus' name, I ask You to bind the powers of the evil one and loose Your kingdom here on earth as it is in Heaven.*

MY DAILY JOURNAL

DELIVER US – DAY SEVEN

In the Old Testament, the nation of Judah was surrounded by multiple nations. War was imminent. After seeking God for direction, the Lord said to King Jehoshaphat, "Do not be afraid nor dismayed because of this great multitude, for the battle is not yours, but God's" (2 Chronicles 20:15 NKJV).

As they chose to praise God in the middle of their circumstance, He set an ambush against their enemies and the victory was won completely and overwhelmingly (2 Chronicles 20:22). The key moment in the story was when Judah realized and acknowledged that it wasn't their battle. The battle was the Lord's.

When we truly believe that our battle belongs to God, we can confidently keep our focus on Him rather than our problems. We can find perfect peace as we rest in His power to deliver, no matter the scope of our struggle. How? By remembering this simple truth: The size of the battle is never too big for us when compared to the size of our God!

PRAY: *Father, I know there's nothing that will oppose me today that can't be conquered through Your strength. The battle is not mine, it's Yours!*

MY DAILY JOURNAL

CONCLUSION

We hope you've enjoyed this amazing journey of prayer over the past six weeks. We pray it's been life-changing and that the effects will be seen in your life for years to come.

However, we also trust this is not the end but rather only the beginning of an even richer prayer experience. May you feel an increased daily measure of the Holy Spirit's presence as you continually put into practice what you've learned by studying the Lord's Prayer. May God continue to give you new and deeper revelation into the supernatural power of a consistent prayer and devotional life. May we all hunger for it like a deer thirsts for water.

We truly believe that no matter the question, the answer can be found in prayer. It may come right away or it may take some persistence, but God is waiting for you right now. You only need to take the time to pray.

Small Group Resources

Group Roster

Group Guidelines

Prayer & Praise Report

For more resources on small groups visit

SmallGroupChurches.com

Small Group Roster

NAME	PHONE	EMAIL

Small Group Guidelines

It's a good idea for everyone to put words to their shared values, expectations and commitments. Such guidelines will help avoid unspoken agendas and unmet expectations. We recommend you discuss your guidelines during Session One to lay the foundation for a healthy group experience. Feel free to modify anything that doesn't work for your group.

WE AGREE TO THESE VALUES:

CLEAR PUPROSE	To grow healthy spiritual lives by building a healthy small group community.
GROUP ATTENDANCE	To give priority to the group meeting (call if absent or late)
SAFE ENVIRONMENT	To create a safe place where people can be heard and feel loved (no quick answers, snap judgments or simple fixes)
BE CONFIDENTIAL	To keep anything that is shared strictly confidential within the group

CONFLICT RESOLUTION — To avoid gossip and immediately resolve concerns by following the principles of Matthew 18:15-17

SPIRITUAL HEALTH — To give group members permission to speak into my life and help me live a healthy, balanced spiritual life

LIMIT OUR FREEDOM — To limit our freedom by not serving or consuming alcohol during group activities so as to avoid causing a weaker member to stumble (1 Cor. 8:1-13; Romans 14:19-21)

WELCOME NEWCOMERS — To invite friends who might benefit from this study and warmly welcome newcomers

SCRIPTURE — While everyone's thoughts and opinions are valuable and encouraged, to ultimately rely on the truth of Scripture as our final authority

BUILDING RELATIONSHIPS — To get to know the other members of the group and pray for them regularly

Prayer & Praise Report

This is a place where you can write each other's requests for prayer. You can also make a note when God answers a prayer. Pray for each other's requests. If you're new to group prayer, it's okay to pray silently or to pray by using just one sentence:

"God, please help _____ to _____."

DATE	PERSON	PRAYER REQUEST	PRAISE

FORTY DAYS OF PRAYER

ABOUT REAL LIFE CHURCH

The vision for a church that looks like heaven has been developing in the hearts of our leadership team for years. In 2005, the Hagan family moved to the Natomas area of Sacramento and begin to lay the groundwork for Real Life Church, originally known as Mars Hill Community Church. A core group of families began to gather as they learned and embraced the vision, meeting on Thursday nights to plan, learn and grow in relationship. Word spread about an exciting new church about to begin and the core group prepared for opening day.

January 8, 2006 was the official launch date for Real Life and the morning was historic. As we came together as authentic family, the Spirit of God was present and we celebrated as He changed people's lives. From that first morning at American Lakes Elementary, we have been blessed to be a part of God's plan and the redeeming power of His love.

During our first year, God was already growing the seeds of our first church plant. The Yarbrough family had moved back to California, and had been attending Real Life Arena Campus while a core group was built in Fairfield. In March, 2007 just 14 months after the opening of our first location, our second campus, Real Life Church of Fairfield, was born. Just two years later, in the spring of 2009, our Fairfield Campus gave birth to another ministry, Fairfield Christian School, which is now the only dual accredited, K-12 Christian School in the city of Fairfield.

Then, in October of 2009, our Arena campus moved to a permanent church home at 1921 Arena Blvd. The building has been completely remodeled, and God's blessings and provision through His people have created an amazing place!

Apparently God wasn't done because while we were moving into our Arena location, God was speaking to the hearts of the Seiler family about moving to Galt and launching our 3rd campus. In May of 2010, Real Life Church of Galt became a reality. After just 3 years, we've moved into a newly remodeled facility that will also serve as a Community Center throughout the week, reaching the local families with the good news of Jesus.

Next, in March 2014, we launched Real Life Church Artisan Campus in Northern Sacramento. Then, in March 2015 came our first out-of-state campus, Anthem of Hope, in Columbus, Ohio. August, 2015 brought the launch of Natomas Christian School at our Arena campus. Just one month later, Real Life Church of West Sacramento was born.

We are overwhelmed at God's faithfulness as we look back over the past 10 years. Looking ahead, God is still opening doors and we're still walking through them. We are filled with faith and trusting in His wisdom and provision as we endeavor to make Real Life Church a place that is deeply engaged in our communities, spreading the message of God's love from neighborhoods to nations.

Made in the USA
Columbia, SC
13 March 2020